HUMAN IMPACT ON EARTH: CAUSE AND EFFECT

CHANGING RAIN FOREST ENVIRONMENTS

TANYA DELLACCIO

PowerKiDS
press

New York

Published in 2020 by The Rosen Publishing Group, Inc.
29 East 21st Street, New York, NY 10010

First Edition

Editor: Jane Katirgis
Book Design: Reann Nye

Photo Credits: Series art Xiebiyun/Shutterstock.com; Alexander Tolstykh/Shutterstock.com; Cafe Racer/Shutterstock.com; cover Posnov/Moment Open/Getty Images; p. 5 Kunlaphat Raksakul/Shutterstock.com; p. 6 2009fotofriends/Shutterstock.com; p. 7 LeoFFreitas/Moment Open/Getty Images; p. 8 DR Travel Photo and Video/Shutterstock.com; p. 9 https://commons.wikimedia.org/wiki/File:Thismia_rodwayi_(Fairy_lantern)_2.JPG; p. 10 CPbackpacker/Shutterstock.com; p. 11 Stanislav71/Shutterstock.com; p. 13 David Tipling/DigitalVision/Getty Imges; pp. 14, 15 AFP/Getty Images; p. 17 luoman/E+/Getty Images; p. 18 Petr Klabal/Shutterstock.com; p. 19 DE AGOSTINI PICTURE LIBRARY/De Agostini/Getty Images; pp. 20, 21 ERNESTO BENAVIDES/AFP/Getty Images; p. 23 Mattias Klum/National Geographic Image Collection/Getty Images; p. 24 Nuttawut Uttamaharad/Shutterstock.com; p. 25 ullstein bild/Getty Images; p. 26 Quick Shot/Shutterstock.com; p. 27 Anadolu Agency/Getty Images; p. 29 Richard Whitcombe/Shutterstock.com; p. 30 L. Toshio Kishiyama/Moment/Getty Images.

Library of Congress Cataloging-in-Publication Data

Names: Dellaccio, Tanya, author.
Title: Changing rain forest environments / Tanya Dellaccio.
Description: New York : PowerKids Press, [2020] | Series: Human impact on
   Earth: cause and effect | Includes index.
Identifiers: LCCN 2019001032| ISBN 9781725301368 (paperback) | ISBN
   9781725301382 (library bound) | ISBN 9781725301375 (6 pack)
Subjects: LCSH: Rain forest ecology—Juvenile literature. | Climatic
   changes—Juvenile literature. | Nature—Effect of human beings
   on—Juvenile literature.
Classification: LCC QH541.5.R27 D47 2020 | DDC 577.34—dc23
LC record available at https://lccn.loc.gov/2019001032

Manufactured in the United States of America

CPSIA Compliance Information: Batch #CSPK19. For Further Information contact Rosen Publishing, New York, New York at 1-800-237-9932.

CONTENTS

HELPING US SURVIVE

Rain forests are beautiful **ecosystems** filled with tens of thousands of different plants and animals. There are many kinds of rain forests, each with different characteristics. Generally, rain forests are very humid and very warm.

These ecosystems provide humans with many resources that help us survive. Rain forests absorb carbon dioxide from the environment and release oxygen. Many resources, like oxygen, are naturally occurring, meaning humans don't have to do any work to benefit from them. Other resources such as products coming from mining and farming require a bit of work from humankind. The human impact to **retrieve** some of these resources has put rain forest ecosystems in danger and negatively affected the plants and animals that live there.

IMPACT FACTS

Even though rain forests only cover about 6 percent of Earth's land, they play an important role in regulating Earth's climate by producing oxygen and contributing to the water cycle.

More than half of the world's known species can be found in Earth's tropical rain forests.

TEMPERATE AND TROPICAL

There are generally two types of rain forests. The first type is a tropical rain forest, which has average temperatures ranging from 70°F to 85°F (21°C to 30°C). Because of the humidity, tropical rain forests get a lot of rain, up to 400 inches (1,016 cm) per year. The second type is a temperate rain forest, with cooler average temperatures of 40 to 54°F (4 to 12°C). Temperate rain forests average about 100 inches (250 cm) per year.

ALL OVER THE WORLD

Rain forests can be found near Earth's equator, which is an imaginary line splitting Earth into two **hemispheres**—Northern and Southern. Most rain forests are situated in the lower part of North America, the upper part of South America, the middle part of Africa, and parts of Asia and Australia.

FOUR LAYERS

There are four different layers to each rain forest—emergent, canopy, understory, and forest floor. The emergent layer is made from the tops of very tall trees. Since it's at the top, it gets the most sunlight. The canopy is right below the emergent layer and has thick leaves. Below that is the understory, which is very humid. The final layer is the forest floor, which is very dark and therefore doesn't have many plants that grow there.

Because of all the rain in the rain forests, they hold a lot of fresh water. The Amazon rain forest holds 20 percent of Earth's fresh water.

The most important rain forest is the Amazon rain forest, which is located in northern South America. It's the largest rain forest in the world. It spans 2,300,000 square miles (6,000,000 sq km) and occupies 40 percent of Brazil. It's located at the **drainage basin** of the Amazon River, giving it the perfect conditions for a flourishing ecosystem. Tens of thousands of different plants and animals live there—and they all serve an important purpose.

OXYGEN AROUND THE WORLD

There are many thousands of plant species that call rain forests home. About two-thirds of the plant species in the world can be found there.

Due to human impacts, more than half of the world's tropical rain forests have been destroyed since 1947.

The Amazon rain forest alone holds around 40,000 different plant species. More than half of those species are important in **sustaining** different processes not only in the rain forest, but also around the world. They provide a source of food for the animals living there. On a larger scale, however, they release oxygen through **photosynthesis**, which helps make the environment livable. Due to the unique climate, many plants that grow in rain forests aren't found anywhere else in the world.

PLANTS AND PEOPLE

When you think of a rain forest, you probably think of big green trees and large winding vines. If you look closer, though, you'll see other types of plants, too. Flowers, such as orchids, are especially **abundant** in the rain forest.

Humans have found many plants from the rain forest and taken them home to **cultivate**. Orchids are an example of a plant that originally came from tropical rain forests.

Some plants will only grow in the rain forest. The Brazil nut tree, for example, won't grow anywhere else. This means its fruit needs to be harvested directly from the rain forest.

Humans benefit a great deal from plants in the rain forests. Many of the plants have been found to have **medicinal** properties. This means they can help treat illnesses, including cancer. Of the many plants that scientists have found over the years that can help treat cancer, 70 percent of them are from the rain forest. With scientists discovering more than 2,000 new plant species all over the world every year, imagine how many beneficial species are still yet to be found!

ANIMALS HELPING OUT

Plants aren't the only things living in the rain forest—thousands of animal species make their home there, too. Animals ranging in size from gigantic elephants to tiny ants help keep Earth's rain forest ecosystems thriving.

Since there are four different levels of a rain forest, there are four completely different ecosystems for the animals living there. Many animals never cross into another level. They help regulate the ecosystem by spreading seeds, helping more plants grow. Spider monkeys, which can be found in the canopy level of the Amazon rain forest, play an important role in spreading seeds throughout their habitat. This ensures that the plants will continue growing and, in turn, contribute to a balanced and flourishing ecosystem.

FROG FLUIDS

Animals in the rain forest have been found to have medicinal properties, too. Fluids from a poisonous frog in Columbia have properties that can be used as an **anesthetic** or a muscle relaxer. The frog itself is dangerous and very deadly to humans. But when its fluids are broken down chemically, they can be used as medicine.

Rain forests are home to a diverse variety of animals. The red-eyed tree frog, shown here, is a common rain forest animal from southern Mexico to northern South America.

CALLING THE RAIN FORESTS HOME

There are many different groups of people who live in and around the rain forests. They both help and hurt the rain forests' survival. Many communities rely on the rain forests for food, hunting the larger animals.

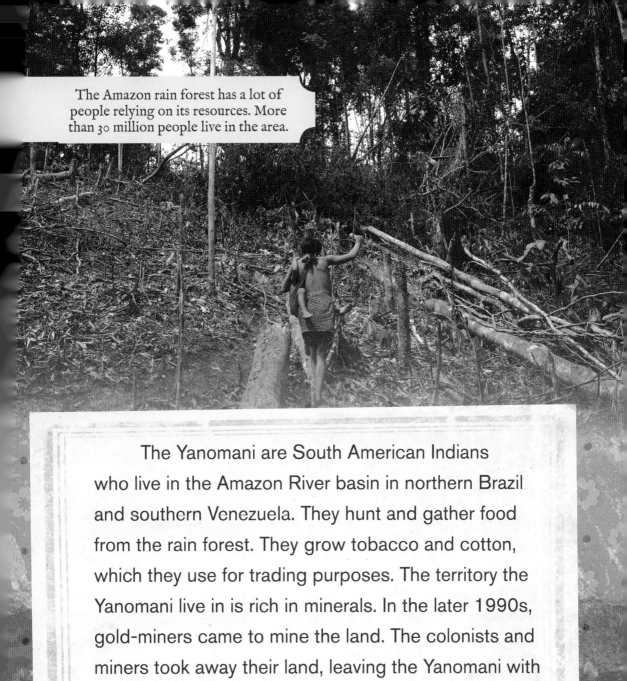

The Amazon rain forest has a lot of people relying on its resources. More than 30 million people live in the area.

The Yanomani are South American Indians who live in the Amazon River basin in northern Brazil and southern Venezuela. They hunt and gather food from the rain forest. They grow tobacco and cotton, which they use for trading purposes. The territory the Yanomani live in is rich in minerals. In the later 1990s, gold-miners came to mine the land. The colonists and miners took away their land, leaving the Yanomani with only 30 percent of their original territory. Many other communities of the rain forest are at risk of losing their homeland, too.

DEVASTATING DEFORESTATION

It's easy to think of the world's rain forests as functioning, healthy ecosystems that are home to thousands of plants and animals. Unfortunately, many of these plants and animals are dying because of human interactions with their homes.

Deforestation is the removal of Earth's forests for human benefit. It's a growing problem around the world, and its effects are becoming increasingly concerning. Logging, mining, and farming are the three biggest reasons our world's rain forests are crumbling. The deforestation of rain forests causes many different ecological changes, and each change causes a chain reaction for another species. Some of these effects are immediate, but some take a long time to make an impact.

It is estimated that if deforestation in Earth's rain forests continues at such a rapid rate, every 10 years between 5 and 10 percent of the species that live there will disappear. >

17

CHAIN REACTION

Logging is when people cut down mass amounts of trees. The wood is used for many different purposes, such as constructing buildings or making paper. There are many negative impacts of logging.

The most immediate impact is the destruction of ecosystems that are home to plants and animals. Cutting down trees destroys not only the plants but also the food and shelter the animals rely on to survive.

Logging solely for the purpose of collecting wood does a lot of damage to the rain forests. Unfortunately, a lot of times, logging is just the first step to other harmful human impacts.

Some impacts of logging take longer to occur. Research has shown that certain rain forest trees won't grow back after they've been cut down. Even years after the logging of a specific area, that part of the rain forest may not grow back, and its inhabitants may not return.

DANGEROUS DIGGING

Mining helps people retrieve different minerals from Earth. Many of those minerals, such as gold, copper, tin, and nickel, can be found in Earth's rain forests. Digging deep into the ground to find them, however, is a great strain on rain forest ecosystems. Some of the minerals even release harmful gases into the air. Explosives are often used to create mining holes, which releases dangerous chemicals and harms the plants and animals nearby.

The rain forests in Peru are at great risk of being eliminated completely because of mining. The photographs on pages 20 and 21 show the destruction caused by an illegal gold mining project in La Pampa, Peru, in 2015.

It's not just digging into the ground that makes mining practices in the rain forest so threatening. Miners cut down trees to create roads to access their dig sites, causing more destruction to the ecosystems. Much of the mining in rain forests is illegal.

OLD LAND, NEW CROPS

Because rain forests offer good temperatures and large plots of land for farming, large areas are cut down to make room for **agricultural** purposes. "Slash-and-burn" agriculture is a type of farming that involves cutting down and burning large patches of land to make a fresh start for plants to grow.

Plants rely on nutrients from their surroundings to grow. When people use the slash-and-burn method, the soil left after the fires go out is initially good for planting crops. But only a few plantings are successful in the newly cleared area, meaning the land becomes useless after a couple of years.

This photo shows the aftermath of the slash-and-burn process in a rain forest in Malaysia. >

23

OIL PROBLEMS

Oil extraction is a big problem facing both the rain forests and the people who live near them. Companies search rain forests for oil reserves and begin the process of drilling and destroying the land to retrieve them. One of the biggest threats of this process is the toxic waste released into the environment that harms plants, animals, and people living in the area.

PALM OIL TREES

PALM OIL

Palm oil is a vegetable oil collected from the fruits of palm trees in rain forests of Malaysia and Indonesia. It has many different uses, one of which is its use as cooking oil and an ingredient in many processed foods. It's also used in many different products, such as cosmetics. Rain forests are facing extreme deforestation due to the cultivation of palm oil trees. Organizations such as the Rain Forest Alliance have teamed up with farmers and businesses to provide an ecofriendly way to harvest palm oil.

Oil production in a rain forest of Ecuador is destructive to the ecosystem.

Even the initial search for oil causes a lot of damage. For example, roads need to be paved for searchers to come in, and they need to be big enough for their drilling equipment. Mass deforestation occurs because of this. Many harmful oil drilling practices have been made illegal in an attempt to lessen the impact on the rain forests.

CLIMATE CHANGE

Deforestation of rain forests is causing more damage than we think—it's a big factor in climate change. Because so much carbon dioxide is released into our atmosphere, Earth's temperature is rising. About 25 percent of the world's carbon resides in tropical rain forests. Many factors cause climate change, but since trees hold a lot of carbon, cutting them down in rain forests significantly contributes to the increased release of carbon.

IMPACT FACTS

Organizations such as Conservation International research natural areas that are in danger and help find solutions to keep their ecosystems thriving.

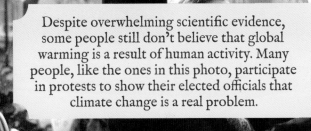

Despite overwhelming scientific evidence, some people still don't believe that global warming is a result of human activity. Many people, like the ones in this photo, participate in protests to show their elected officials that climate change is a real problem.

STOP DENYING OUR EARTH IS DYING

In addition, climate change can alter rain forests. Since the temperature is rising, rainfall can decrease, causing droughts. This not only threatens the animals and growth of plants living there but also can cause huge forest fires. Luckily, environmental organizations help to decrease these effects.

FINDING A BALANCE

There's an important balance between saving Earth's rain forests and collecting the materials we need to survive. There's no way to completely ensure the preservation of rain forests, but there are ways to safely extract resources while doing as little harm as possible.

Logging destruction can be minimized by using practices that help map out the area of land before the trees are harvested. Responsible companies research and study the area where trees are going to be cut down. They test the soil and plan out the best time of year to harvest trees in order to do the least amount of damage. Planning out the best route to pave roads for workers and machinery can help minimize the deforestation during logging, too.

Palm oil plantations, such as this one in Thailand, impact the native plants and animals of a rain forest. Future human activities must focus on minimizing damage to rain forests. >

HOW WE CAN HELP

One of the biggest things we can do to help limit the destruction of the world's rain forests is be aware of where our products are coming from. Buying things such as recycled paper products or ethically sourced gold can help minimize the deforestation of the rain forests. Equally as important is to stop buying things that lead to rain forest destruction. Check the ingredients labels of foods you or your family often eat to see whether palm oil is an ingredient. You can have an impact on the environment when you decide what to buy.

There are several organizations dedicated to preserving rain forests. The World Wildlife Fund and the Rain Forest Alliance are two examples. They are committed to saving our world's rain forests and the plants and animals at risk all over the world. Together, we can keep the world's rain forests safe.

GLOSSARY

abundant: Existing in large amounts.

agricultural: Producing crops.

anesthetic: A substance that causes a person to be insensitive to pain. It is often used during surgery or dental procedures.

cultivate: To raise crops by caring for the land and plants as they grow.

drainage basin: A place where rain collects.

ecosystem: A natural community of living and nonliving things.

hemisphere: One-half of Earth.

inhabitant: A person who lives somewhere.

medicinal: Used to relieve pain.

parasite: A living thing that lives in, on, or with another living thing and often harms it.

photosynthesis: The process in which plants make energy.

retrieve: To bring back.

sustain: To help support a process and keep it going.

INDEX

WEBSITES

Due to the changing nature of Internet links, PowerKids Press has developed an online list of websites related to the subject of this book. This site is updated regularly. Please use this link to access the list: www.powerkidslinks.com/HIOE/rainforest